A Spiritual Code of Ethics

by

Ann Coon

Copyright © 2009
by Ann Coon

Printed in the United States of America.
All rights reserved.
First printing 10-2009

No part of this book may be reproduced in any form or by any means, without the written permission of the publisher.

ISBN: 978-0-9786202-4-0
       0-9786202-4-0

Library of Congress Control Number: 2009930602

Published by
Inkwell Productions
10869 N. Scottsdale Road #103-128
Scottsdale, AZ 85254-5280
Phone (480) 315-3781
Email: info@inkwellproductions.com
Website: www.inkwellproductions.com

CONTENTS

Acknowledgment vii
Author – A Master Voice

Dedication ix

Prologue xi

The Beatitudes* xv

Psalm 100 xvii

CHAPTERS

1. "A Spiritual Code of Ethics" 1
   Give To Give
   Be Not Afraid to Follow Your Heart and Give of Your Gifts

2. A Simple Explanation Why The Open Heart is the Doorway to Heaven 7

3. This Is A New Lesson to New Beginners 9
   Trusting Is the Way of the Lord

4. The Art of Forgiving 13
   We Get to Choose the Garden That We Plant Our Seeds In, Being Free of Other People's Choices; Looking In, Not Out

5. The Loving Self-Loving Nature 19
   What Does It Mean Not to Accept the Past As a Partner?

6. Love One Another As I Have Loved You 23
   Giving Away Gentleness As a Gift From the Unconditional Heart

7. Awakening to the Spirit of Time 27

8. Dearest Ones, July 14, 2004 29

Epilogue: The Marriage Within 31
Ann's personal letter/prayer to her Lord and her God

---

* Includes: Blessed are they who teach of my ways with good intentions.

Acknowledgment

Author – A Master Voice

I am grateful to have received of these words from My Beloved Lord and God. I am pleased to return a favor. His Life, His Word, has placed a new meaning in my life, for now I give what I have received: the gifts of forgiveness and kindness.

Thank you to all who made this book possible; family, friends and a special thank you to Nick Ligidakis for taking his part in honoring the plan.

Dedication

I wish to dedicate this book to those who have treated their heart, my heart. Time is coming onto planet Earth where all hearts will rejoice with the coming – "The Second Coming." God has granted a choice pair to enter His Kingdom of Love, of Loving, before all others. They went through the trials and tribulations of our dear planet and wish now to share their heart's glory upon this Earth we now inhabit. Dedication to this book "A Spiritual Code of Ethics," just "Give to Give" is already in progress.

Ann has willed this beautiful book to those who have gone before her, those that have lighted the pathway that she was chosen to take so that many eyes and many hearts will be lifted when the curtain to the New World is brought down. Then love will emanate from the heart of the planet so that those in the time now will feel the need to procreate their thoughts and bring about a lasting peace, a lasting joy. Time ushers in new literature, new paintings, new sculptures, and new ways of feeding the people of the chosen race.

We, Ann and I, her Master Lord and God, wish to send to each and every heart a feeling of being well blessed with God's good nature. Centered in God's willingness to serve the Lord in each and every one of us and that Lord serves the God force that will bring about the necessary change. God is willing, be that for you.

MY PARENTS

John and Winifred Kovolenus

Prologue

Thank you for allowing me to come into your life, your heart. I wish to introduce this woman, Ann, to you. There are many of you who know of me and many who do not. For those who are wondering why and how this beautiful book fell into my hands, I wish to share a most profound experience with you that set me on this "Miraculous Course" – my path.

My mother, Winifred Kovolenus, was a remarkable woman. She shared with me her pains and her sorrows of doing her work in the prison of the mind. You see, Mother was an abused child of society's teachings. She was never given the opportunity to witness to others her true self. She wanted to share her life, her story, with someone, and I am truly graced by the fact I was chosen. Mother was labeled "paranoid schizophrenic" early in her 40's. In fact, it all began after her first son died in her arms at six months of age.

I was the last of six children born to John and Winifred Kovolenus in 1944, in a small northeastern Pennsylvania town, Clark's Summit. Clark's Summit is just outside of the Scranton Wilkes-Barre area, a region known for its coal mines. Both parents were of Lithuanian descent. We had what the world called "humble roots." My father worked the coal mines for 49 years. My mother worked equally hard throughout her years, even those years while placed in a mental hospital!

I had a very good reason to find "a mother" for me early in my life to sustain my goal of parenting me and caring for me. I chose to see the Blessed Mother Mary as my spiritual mother; her character, her gentleness, her strength, her wisdom stood by me as it does now. She wanted very much for me to follow Her Son and His teachings. I didn't realize it at the time, but my life would run a parallel course with Winifred. My mind was set early in life to find out who and what took her away so early, away from the good she deserved and the mother I really wanted to know.

As spirit would have it, I entered nurses training in 1962 at age 17 and graduated three years later as a registered nurse. I am thankful for the path that was set before me. I got to love and serve more. From the marriage in 1966 came two beautiful children: Christopher and Deborah, the picture of the little ones you see in the book. Once again I was given the opportunity to love and serve more.

Whenever I could throughout my married life, I took Mother with me sometimes a few weeks, or a few months at a time wanting to share my "good life" with her. I treated her as my mother and me the daughter, not wanting to mother my mother. She deserved more. She deserved respect. I wanted to give back to her the respect she couldn't give to herself.

After my fathers passing, Mother had to enter a nursing home. Nothing seemed to give mother peace, a lasting peace, that is: the peace that she so deserved. I can remember traveling to the nursing home one particular day, and as I was driving, I said to my Lord, "Tell me Lord what can I do for her? I don't know what else to do." A voice said to me, "Love her." Now it is nearly 45 years since her illness.

Throughout her life, for as long as I can remember, she continuously asked for forgiveness, and as she grew weaker the request became stronger. She was begging to be forgiven. I knew it was time to take this forgiveness seriously. She indeed was stretching out her hand for forgiveness to happen, to give to her the peace that she needed. I knew the regrets she had in her life; I felt them for her. She couldn't release the torment from her mind – the past was tormenting her. She couldn't remove "the stone" before her.

I remember a day that will never be forgotten, the day I entered the nursing home. I went to her room, sat down beside her and took her fragile hands into mine. Looking into the deep wells of her eyes, our souls connected like never before, and we forgave one another. I said, "Mother, will you forgive me for any wrong I might have done to you?" Then I told her, "I forgive you for any wrong you might have done to me." I went on to tell her that all I saw was one of the most beautiful women I had ever seen, and I was proud to be her daughter. She was pure; she was innocent. I indeed saw an angel before me. God was there witnessing two women coming face to face with their true identity: "mother." It was through that miracle called "forgiveness" – forgive to be forgiven, that life at that moment took on a new meaning for me. Within a short time she passed on, but before she did, I came into her room and sang to her the beautiful song "Gentle Woman." She said in a clear voice, "Ann, is that you?" When I said yes, she told me something profound: "Someone is going to write a book about me."

My life as I see it now has been an awesome experience. At the time of going through life's experiences, its pains, its sorrows, I found myself sitting with the pain to heal with it. I now can lean back into my heart space, where my loving father is waiting for me to come rest awhile. I know now my human life experience was meant to be for me to find true humbleness. Yes, life does have a way of causing us to humble ourselves to a strength, and wisdom greater than can be seen and felt by the human self alone. Divine self gives you a gentle strength and a gentle wisdom, and that is where God and goddess are united as one.

Thank you, dear reader, for coming into this place and time with me, and do enjoy my Master's thoughts as I have received them.

The Beatitudes*

And seeing the multitudes, He went up on a mountain,
And when He was seated, His disciples came to Him.
Then He opened His mouth and taught them, saying:

> Blessed *are* the poor in spirit,
> For theirs is the kingdom of heaven.
>
> Blessed *are* those that mourn,
> For they shall be comforted.
>
> Blessed *are* the meek,
> For they shall inherit the earth.
>
> Blessed *are* those who hunger and thirst for righteousness,
> For they shall be filled.
>
> Blessed *are* the merciful,
> For they shall obtain mercy.
>
> Blessed *are* the pure in heart,
> For they shall see God.
>
> Blessed *are* the peacemakers,
> For they shall be called sons of God.
>
> Blessed *are* those who are persecuted for righteousness' sake,
> For theirs is the kingdom of heaven.

Blessed *are* you when men shall revile and
persecute you,
And say all kinds of evil against you falsely for My sake.

Blessed are they who teach of My ways with good intention.**

Rejoice and be exceedingly glad, for great is your reward in heaven,
For so they persecuted the prophets who were before you.

*Schuller & Dunn /The New Possibility Thinkers Bible
Thomas Nelson Publisher /1996
**Ann Coon/Her Brother Jesus

Psalm 100

A Psalm of Thanksgiving

Make a joyful shout to the Lord,
All you lands!

Serve the Lord with Gladness;
Come before His presence with singing.

Know that the Lord, He is God;
It is He who has made us, and not we ourselves;
We are His people and the sheep of His pasture.

Enter into His gates with thanksgiving,
And into His courts with praise.
Be thankful to Him, and bless His name.

For the Lord is good;
His mercy is everlasting,
And His truth endures to all generations.

1

A Spiritual Code of Ethics: Give To Give

This will be a new book on golden principles on which to live with. None other has been printed as this, and none other will. We will take a short walk together to where we as partners coming into this life took off a long time ago… You were asked to obey your Father's will for you. Many have forgotten to do so. Few have stayed on the path to follow these principles. Let us not forget to keep the path open from getting cluttered with what's "out there." We must keep focused on what is inside to pay attention to.

Life was not meant to be a mystery. Life was meant to be solved, so that we/you can live a happy and profitable life. Many have forgotten what a profitable life is on earth. Profits have nothing to do with the stock market nor the money laying in the bank vaults. You have misunderstood the intentions of wealth and the wealthy. You must give of your wealth with good intentions to receive more wealth. This is not only true of your physical wealth; it is equally true of your spiritual wealth. Spiritual wealth demands of you to give of it, to spend it, to make sure you have it for yourself. Too many have fallen short of this simple rule. You must receive to give in the spiritual world. If you have not given of your gifts, you will not know you have the gift.

Love is an honorable thing and wishes to be used according to its fruits. Apples cannot produce of "other people's apples." You must choose if you are willing to follow these simple rules: to select the vine-ripened apples and give them freely and without charge, otherwise the giving cannot be realized by yourself or the recipient. "Give to Give" is the key phrase. There are times coming upon you that all that was not given will be taken away and redistributed to the charities, those in need of the fruit, as others have not shared their fruit with them.

Be careful of my words; they are spoken in truth. Hear these in truth. Love is not to be tampered with. It is to be given freely and without charge. Never before has real wealth been asked for in a country so rich, and yet a country who has spent its gifts most unwisely. It asks to receive something for what it has given. There is no truth in this and never has been. Be aware of those with peace treaties who wish to embellish their own souls. God asks nothing more of you but to give to receive. It is better to give, for you come to see the just reward of giving; you get to receive the gift. Some will doubt these words and feel these words are made up, but I ask you why would you think these words false when they have been handed down through the ages and they have worked. Renaissance times have proven of this very thing. Beautiful art was displayed all over His

Kingdom of beautiful messages of wealth, the real wealth we are now discussing. Get out of your heads the idea that this thought which I have spoken to you of "Give to Give" does not work, for it is the only thing that works. Society cannot function without this "Give to Give."

This is a new license given to new partnerships; a heart worth living is a heart worth dying for. Many have done this in this day and age. Many have bent over backwards to get the system to work, and yet many are not willing to give of their famous possessions, their hard earned money. They keep their wealth in their back pocket, just in case the right person comes around to give it to. The next person is sent to you, and yet you fail to receive because you fail to give of yourself and your riches. You hide them as if the moths would get into your pockets and devour them. Much has gone on in the world of riches recently that dismays the spiritually-minded. Their minds become gray and dismal while other minds become full of light but to find out their riches have been snatched up "out of their pocket," the pocket that was intended for them, for they understood what "Give to Give" meant.

Be honest with yourself, if you are not abiding with this common rule, you are banking in the wrong bank! Life will pass by while you wait at the street corner with your fortunes tucked inside of your heart, never having given them away. You are being asked to give up those treasures, so the world will lighten of the load that the previous generations have left, simply misunderstood of the simple rule "Give to Give." Few are going among you proud to have understood this rule despite the many dangers they have concealed within their open hearts.

The doorway to heaven is through the open heart; it cannot get through with bags of forgotten treasures tied to your girth. The time is now to go within your own heart and to see the infractions that you have placed upon yourself, not seeing the need of your brothers/sisters holding out their hands to you asking for nothing more than forgiveness, for they have not received of your gifts of forgiveness and kindness.

Behold those who see the needs of the world and have not blocked their vision and give what is left of their treasures, no matter how small their remaining treasures are. I ask you kind people be generous to one another, careful not to impress others with your good deeds and their misdeeds. Punishment is not a gift. It is a gift of the poor-hearted, those who have reaped of "others rewards." Be careful of those sudden storms that come in your daily life and tempt you to give up your place in heaven's consciousness to those responsible for those sudden storms. Place yourself in the middle of the boat, and ride the waves till the storms pass. Grant others immunity always, free access to your heart's door when life has shut the door on them. Be careful that you do not keep the door closed on the lover waiting on the other side, for he too is looking for safe refuge. Many have knocked but have been refused an opening to your heart's door. Our hearts are connected by a fine thread; words of comfort and solace are words that heal the wounded. No one needs to know what they have done wrong; they seek from a comforting heart. Won't you be that comforting heart? A kind look, a gentle smile, a tender hug are your greatest resources to your brothers/sisters.

A Spiritual Code of Ethics

Be not afraid to give of your gifts. These gifts have been given to you as gifts. Gifts are then dispersed to those in need not the wealthy, those who already have my gifts and wish not to share them. Thus it is in your favor to leave all of your treasures here on earth while you live. Give to the broken-hearted; don't take from the broken-hearted. Give to those sealed in darkness your light. Give to those with deafened ears your smile, and they will hear again. God's word needs less to be spoken and more to be given.

A Spiritual Code of Ethics

Practical Application for Chapter 1

Be Not Afraid to Follow Your Heart and Give of Your Gifts

We as humans go through birth cycles so we can experience the cycles of energies to produce more "new" energy. Moving away from the old, worn-out pathways; paths that do not produce new energy, energies that energize are a necessity for true growing and true giving. Give yourself room to grow, room to expand. Listening to your heart's desire is always the way to increase growth and soul's contentment. Another's heart need not be broken if truth is always at the forefront. This is what "A Spiritual Code of Ethics" is all about.

As a mother of earth, the only way my mother could teach me of my worth was to allow me to feel my womanhood and to appreciate the gifts that I bring to my altar of life and to the altar of life of others. Giving myself the loving kindness that is required on a daily basis; to illuminate my life, to keep her power…her energy aglow.

2

A Simple Explanation of Why the Open Heart is The Doorway to Heaven

Remember my words. Ye must come through me to achieve lasting peace, or the doorway will be closed until you take the rags off your back and the stones in your purse and grant me your thoughts, your words, your actions. Think on these things. I need for you to come in through that door into my heart. My disciples have been among you, standing in front of you, welcoming you in their hearts, my heart. Do not take your blows out upon my disciples, my messengers, for they too weep for the city that is buried in its lost treasures. Be kind to one another, hopeful that your sight upon the rock before you will be placed off to the side where you will find me with arms open wide, welcoming you into my heart.

It is time to come, my brothers, my sisters, to your everlasting treasure here with me in the kingdom that I have prepared for you. Go and list my name in one of your friend's invitations to an open house; a house built on solid rock where no man can defeat the cause; God's creation.

Be it done according to your will, your Father's will for you. There is no need to slaughter the fattened calf; sacrifice is non-important. Your treasures need to be given as the supreme sacrifice to your loving Father.

3

This is a New Lesson to New Beginners

Ye must think through me to be born again. I have answered your prayers by being with you every step of the way. You answer my call when you think of me. My character is born of God self, not man self. I am here to teach thee of my integrity. It is about the utmost kind thoughts, always willing to be there in thought, word, and deed to help thee remember me.

I am your way-shower. I show you the way to your open door, your heart, my heart. Be one with me. I call out to you come closer to my heart, your heart. That is where I reside one with thee, me. I have not forgotten about you. I am still there waiting for a knock on my door. The door is not locked; know that it is always open for you to walk through that door and you will find me waiting to greet you when you arrive. I love to love and give love from my loving self. No one is turned away from me who is honest with your own self. Business deals do not work in my book. I need to know you share your better half with me, not you lesser half. Give to God all your treasures, and He will in turn give you of His treasures.

Give nothing away that should not be given away. God asks that you keep a reserve for yourself so that in times of stress there will be food available to feed your God self, your lamb.

Trust in the ways of the Lord. He will lead you to me in times of trouble. He wishes never to shame His children. Shame is out of the question. Shame does not exist in God's Law. God's Law is hampered by people with ideas that shaming will provide results to get the work done. Shame never gets the work done. Shame hinders the work in progress.

Learn to lend me your ear. Listen closely and intently with what the "just God" is telling you. Love me, your way-shower; love God. God is not simply a figurehead. He is one with power and extreme strength, strength to turn your world around so that the stars in the heavens shine down upon your birthplace. He sees your goodness as I see your goodness. He does not play hide and seek. He stands out in the open with his arms open wide asking nothing more from His children, but to play the game of life with "no hurt/harm" to anyone.

The body is an instrument of peace, is it not? It should be that for everyone you meet, keeping in tune with God's chorus in time. He favors time for all His children. He uses time so that we/you can spend a happy time in heaven on earth. Do not cause your family to falter in their steps. Are we all not earth's family together? Do we not have the same Divine Heritage: to be one with the same God in the same will? We share His Divine Birthplace here on earth.

Go back to your humble ways. Live in joint peace with one another. Ask not from one another what you will/wish not for yourself. One cannot honor another who betrays their own trust. You are believing in a righteous God, one who has all the wealth in the world and wishes to share that wealth and spread it around.

God is here, there, and everywhere. There is no place where God is not. Ask not of yourself something that you are not capable of handling. Time takes time to unravel the old ties that bind. Ye must set yourself free from those old ties and remember where your Father and I reside. We are with you in consciousness not far away as many once thought. We reside in each and every one of you. Our door, heaven's door is open to one and all. Just come as you are, and we will trim the tree together. Too many branches get in the way and brings slow growth. Taking away the unneeded branches brings with it its reward: "everlasting peace." When the branches have been trimmed, the tree is prepared for blossoms, then for ripened fruit. Life is in the tree that you are in. You are of the tree of life. Life is good when the fruit is ripe. It must be given away freely without charge, or the tree will stop producing of its kind. I spoke to you now of giving away freely to regain your wealth. Time produces beautiful produce. An early harvest is coming your way, my way.

Practical Application for Chapter 3

Trusting Is the Way of the Lord

When you come to believe in your heart that your way is best for you, you get to enter a new time where the old time doesn't exist for you anymore.

Let me share with you what this belief in a new way, a new time, did for me. I held strongly to the thought that the "yesterdays" no longer existed and that this day and this moment in time was the only time that existed for me. God is present now. I fastened my "inner eye" to this place in time, no matter what was going on around me, and where those thoughts in my mind were tempting me to go. I remember one Sunday morning when I felt I was powered by this tremendous force and went straight "through the roof." I could see a new heaven with blue skies and white fluffy clouds. I could hear myself say, "I can fly!" It was as if I left a place in time where time no longer exists for me. I had entered a new time zone, so to speak. After coming to in my room, I knew something had happened and it took a great energy for me to re-center myself and to feel the force of gravity beneath my feet. This is an example of an energy change that took place within me, moving from one universe to another.

4

The Art of Forgiving

Many have gone wrong thinking that forgiveness is for them. Forgiveness is for the other soul who needs your hand to be forgiven. Life sets itself straight when one is the forgiver and one is the forgiven. God answers through these people and gives these people superior thoughts to live by. Too many have chosen to be the forgivers and wish not to see their own need to be the forgiven. Life can't go on without this "forgiveness therapy." We hold up another's life when we hold a grievance against them because they have wronged us. How could they right us if forgiveness is not given as the gift? You are responsible for your own forgiveness, are you not? Can you honestly forgive others if you have not looked into your own heart to see what there is to forgive? It is all too easy to look within the other's heart and try to right the wrong they are engaged in. We are fine examples of right and wrong to one another. Stepping in closer to get a better look at the other's miseries and examine their cause is abandoning our own. It is not necessary to pay attention to another's cause; we are to pay attention to our own actions, not another's.

When proper tools are used to gain entrance into someone's heart, no one gets hurt. We then become the recipient of the reward, forgiveness. Forgiveness is always a gift. It reminds us of our own immortality as gift-givers. We don't hold onto the gift for fear others might see us as weak. It is beautiful to forgive, not once, but a lifetime of forgiving is necessary to produce a lifetime of loving. Kindness separates us from the givers and the takers. Those who take from the givers sooner or later must return the gift. Practicing the art of forgiveness is a daily job, is it not? It gives you the opportunity to be in grace, the place where love originates.

Kindness is such a wealthy word, and yet it must be practiced on a daily basis. No one can get through life successfully without giving kindness in the way of thoughts, words, and actions, kindness with good intentions. Kindness without good intentions produces a poor crop, and no one benefits. Nothing grows on those branches. We get to choose what garden we plant our seeds in: the garden of good, where much light and nurturing takes place, or the garden of evil, where darkness and barrenness make up the landscape. That is the choice of will: heaven on earth for self and others or hell on earth for self and others. We get to grant the wish. What we will, what we wish for others will eventually show up in our lifescape. The law of "give to give" is the law to abide by, the bank to bank in. You get to choose; that is the freedom of free will. No one can make that choice for you. Free will is a beautiful gift; you get to choose. You get to reap the reward of the choice.

Time answers all prayers in the order that they are received. They cannot be heard unless they come from the heart, true heart, begotten not made, One in Being with The Father, the genuine heart. There is no fruit of evil; the tree is barren. Time wishes to honor time when forgiveness is at the root. Life works, as it should when forgiveness is planted early in that root system. You get to reap its reward: peace and harmony. A life where forgiveness is at the root can make such a difference in another's life. Where there is light there is life, and where there is life, there is forgiveness. I showed you the way to everlasting peace. I said, "Come follow me, my ways." Grant others their way; perhaps it isn't my way, your way. Granting others their way is allowing others free will. It doesn't mean we are to give up our free will to walk the road of our choosing. Benefits arise when partners are free to choose.

Love answers all prayers. It is the way to the heart. Sending messages from the heart to those we meet is in tune with love's creations. We get to reap the reward of increased peace and harmony on our earth and in our own life. Sending love from the heart is the only way it reaches to the depth of one's being. Placing yourself in peace, heaven's consciousness, is the way to peaceful coexistence. Love conquers even the cruelest heart and bathes it with the warmth of the sun's rays. Love truly does exist, for it is the only thing that exists. If it isn't of God source it has no external source. Forgiveness sees that external image and it eventually disappears and new life is brought to the surface.

We need tender, kind, and caring hearts to dissolve what isn't real, so the world will become a tender, kinder, and caring place to live. Come to your heart where forgiveness starts. Lovingly remove the old, and replace it with the new. Come back to your heart, my heart, for that is where love exists. Truth begets truth.

Practical Application for Chapter 4

*We Get to Choose the Garden That We
Plant Our Seeds In,
Being Free of Other People's Choices;
Looking In, Not Out*

Things that used to be, that are no longer needed, indicate that the previous choices no longer serve you. There is no need to examine another's choice. Free will is exactly "freedom of will." We all have that freedom. It is a beautiful gift and we do get to reap the reward of our choice. Allowing others their gift of free will is freedom for both. We get to walk the road of our choice and they get to walk the road of theirs.

Let me share with you an example. I purchased a home in New England, one within my budget that I knew I could afford; spiritually as well as physically. Owning a home means upkeep, maintenance, and work. All of this takes money, time, and energy. I soon realized that in order for my life to work for me, I had to give up certain things. I was looking at quality vs. quantity. I chose foods that were best for me; my health as well as my liking. I chose foods that would fit into my physical and spiritual budget. I decided I could do without a microwave. Since I didn't own a computer, cable wasn't necessary. I gave up the need to have wine. I could use that money for something else. Since I lived alone, it was important for me to "go out" to eat, to be with people, with family. I now had some extra money to treat me to what I needed most. Life is about adjusting and readjusting. Life changes and we get to make those changes; those changes that benefit us at the time. We don't need to look at what others are doing. We must keep vigilant in "our watch." Keep in mind what is the healthy choice for you.

5

The Loving Self – Loving Nature

Patience leads to advising oneself of the route to take. It means having a steady thought pattern to make it work and it takes work to make it happen. Questions arise along the path of life that need not be worked out. Ask not why: just love anyway; it's the thing to do. Character is born of asking not why but leaning to the inside to see the greater lesson that is being taught you.

Being in the Holy State of Grace makes one feel alive and forgiven. Forgiveness always for the giver and the receiver. Time allows time to work out the wrinkles in our lives so that the better "you" comes forth. Finding life as it is, not as it should be, produces miracles in one's life. Not accepting the past as a partner can yield much benefit to the risk-taker; always accepting the need for the soul's growth. Triumph comes when the soul feels at rest with self, knowing it has accomplished its goal for the time now. The soul will feel a need to rest a while in the space it has created from its own growth. If the soul resists growth, it will deal with the resistance it feels until it dares to move to more growth and understanding of self.

The need to feel its oneness with mother side, its worthiness impacts others. Dominance does not belong to the spirit. The spirit and soul work hand and hand to produce the life that is fitting for its own growth. No one can fit in another's soul without its permission. The soul chooses its mate until the time when a new mate is required to reach a higher ground. When the soul learns to expel the thought that life can't exist without another, it is aiming for the higher good. The soul sets goals that are individual and must not be held to another. When it is time to release and let go, the other wants nothing more than a good- bye for its own soul's growth. Partners break up for this reason. We must honor the truth that is within us, not the truth within another. Respect for each other's truth is a necessity; always honor your truth, and respect another's. Truth will allow us to free our self from the ties.

The inner chamber of the heart is a sacred place where you, God, and I exist. It is the marriage bed. One needs to be in that sacred place. We go to that sacred bed, the inner chamber, and rely on the inner thoughts that are exchanged between our partnership with our Divine. Living life from the inner chamber, this sacred marriage allows the human being to make choices that will allow the inner marriage to work as well as the outer marriage in time.

Respecting each other's time is a God thing to do. Time spent in lonesomeness will bring about dire results if the other is not believed to be important. Giving others the feeling of non-importance is asking them to "leave life" and be done with it. Please know that you didn't ask to be born; you were chosen to be born.

God grants us the time we need in this life to relieve ourselves of the burdens that have plagued us over the years. Gathering the events of our life, not the events of others, is most important for our human growth. Time does answer all prayers. It takes extreme patience to believe in time as the chosen healer.

Practical Application for Chapter 5

What Does It Mean Not to Accept the Past As a Partner?

Finding life as it is, not as we once thought it should be truly does produce miracles in one's life. Accepting not the ways and thoughts of another, but your ways and your thoughts, is accepting life for you as it should be. When the soul is ready to move on, you will feel resistance at first, a sort of restlessness taking place. This truly is an indication that one or both partners need to break the ties that once existed. The soul is growing when resistance is being felt. When partners break up, leaving with peace is the answer. Each is going for its higher good.

My mother gave me some wonderful advice before her passing, and I will share that with you. She said, "I listened to and believed too many people out there." Her exact words were, "I listened to every Tom, Dick, and Harry." I will use a female name here, Harriet, to make this gender inclusive. We do have the right to our thoughts at the time we are choosing for us. If another choice in thought comes up, we have the right to choose again. Heaven for one is heaven for another. You see, my Mother was not only my angel, she was my mentor.

6

Love One Another As I Have Loved You

*L*ove doesn't come and go; love remains the same, tenants from one building to another building. Love remains; it can't be destroyed, for love is in the spirit. Spirit knows no shame, no guilt. It fears no one's fear. It gives gentleness away as a gift. The gift is from a gentle heart that you and I exist in. We exist in the Father's love. What isn't love will simply pass away, and what is love will remain. Love can't be asked to leave when it isn't time to leave. Love stays on to honor the love in one's self, the love within another's self. Give unto others that love that you so often hide in me. No need to overcome fear with fear. Fear is overcome with love. Love knoweth not fear. Fear cannot be destroyed; it must be transformed by a loving heart, my heart, your heart. Hearts join to find the love the other one has been missing. Two hearts then become one heart.

Hearts are joining all over the world. There are no two hearts when this happens. We all belong to one heart, the center, the heart of God; the heart of man. Within that heart of man is a beautiful heart of woman, thus the two are equal, no one better or lesser of the other. The heart that burns for one burns brighter for the other.

Time is the truce that teaches man of his essence, and that essence comes from woman. To be born into this world we live in requires that we all be born of woman, our earthly mother side. If woman is to remain woman, the woman must truly believe that she is of man, flesh of his flesh and bone of his bone. The two then become joined on the root of the tree of life. No man, no woman, can go it alone without believing in this principle God the Father placed within Him from the beginning of time: remembering woman where you originated and man remembering where you were born, from the womb of woman.

God truly loves his woman, and woman truly loves her man. They become one of the same root. Be done with this business that you man, you woman, can get along without each other. We both have those parts within our hearts. We are equal to each other, not different from each other because of our physical appearance, but one in the same heart, your heart, my heart, God's heart. God is with you as I am with you and will be with you till there is no more time here on earth. Let us live as one heart beating together and find that rhythm that is all your own and honor that rhythm, one huge heart beating to its own rhythm in time. God is within you/me. Where else could God exist?

Practical Application for Chapter 6

Giving Away Gentleness As a Gift From the Unconditional Heart

Not placing conditions onto another's heart leaves both hearts free, free just to be. Leaving the past behind does prove to be a fruitful endeavor. Granting each other the time and space to do the work that was meant to be done requires great patience. The unconditional heart places no dishonor on another's heart. It honors the time that was given so a greater time can be felt in both honored hearts. Honoring your own heart means honoring another's heart. Man and woman alike both have those parts within their heart; a place where gentleness is the resident heart.

A Spiritual Code of Ethics

7

Awakening To The Spirit of Time

This is a new beginning in time NOW that engages the new spirit with old ancient ways of conducting the world; your world is coming into greater strength than ever before.

Ann had reached a time period in her life where she was able to withstand the thoughts of the old time-users. She was given time to return to the time when a child was taken and abused, and she was asked to suffer with its pains. Ann felt the pain of her only child and returned to that place in time to bring it home, back to her time. She placed that wickedness not in the world but in a most profound place, giving it to the heart to resolve any and all wishes to hurt another heart in time NOW. She felt the pain and anguish of this only child and couldn't resist re-entering an old place in time to rescue the child, which she now owns. The child was no longer misused but given a fine warm home to grow and feel loved. Forgiveness of the world's abused child came through the act of forgiveness of the human self. It was carried out in a church exercise on this day, July 04, 2004, in Phoenix, AZ to heal the world's ill's and to replace it with the new thought of becoming a world of gentler souls to inhabit this place she requested to bring in. The healing of one of God's little ones made this day in history a day of new beginning, knowing the female and male heart are still in working order to accomplish such a great task. She has coupled with another warm heart to help her bring this new child into the world this day. Husband and wife heart felt the enormous strain lifted when the child was released and no longer felt abandoned by the world it was born into. It was a day of thanks, when one child's cry was heard, and a thankful heart returned with the child to bless this world we now inherit. God sends His blessings to all hearts that can rescue one single child's heart. Won't that be you? We need to soften the blows to other hearts when hearts are asked to perform such a task.

God know and feels when the child's heart has been freed to find a true Mother's heart wrapped in love by Father's Love.

Centered in forgiveness is God's welcoming call to all who know and understand a child's heart.

8

July 14, 2004

Dearest Ones,

Ann has just surpassed her greatest test to leave the old land behind and is ready to re-enter a new land where love and only love exists. This only love exists because there is one here and another out there who trusted the truest heart that has ever existed and that being The Brother Jesus Heart. He rekindled the flame when it burned so very low, allowing this woman to enter her only sphere in time, that of gentle time. The gentler one will surpass those with harsh mood swings; those who wish their child die not for the sake of goodness but for their own forsakethness.

God has indeed created a choice pair to enter this new day with new hope for this hopeless planet. Heaven's best have been planted with the seed to go forth and multiply not by human kindness alone but entwined with the gentler heart, the Divine Heart. We wish these brethren more time to gain their inner light so that others coming into the new world will live and will be able to see their light grow brighter than ever before. It takes one single heart, a single soul, to go within and depart from an old thinker in time, when a woman's heart was hurt simply because she came out of man and became woman. God's will be done in the new woman of this new century we are now living.

"Time-setters" are already on this planet to usher in this day as no other way. The good of this new earth just became the good of this new land we are here to preserve; lighter with each of our lights on. Ann and I, her Master, The Lord, wish to all good time-setters wealth in this new land that is already here. Man will speak with woman kindly, and woman will speak with man kindly, both being equal in that heart that sustains the good man and the good woman. Love must enter each heart like never before for each new light to burn on brighter to bring the new children here on Mother Earth with Mother here with Ann, her new chosen profession. Being a woman and true to a woman's heart. The day has come to be what it should be; woman for woman heart and man for man heart. Ann and her chosen partner in life can indeed turn within and find light burning brighter because one light chose light on the darkness that befalls the old time- setter. God be willing, let this be for you.

Epilogue: The Marriage Within

*Ann's personal letter/prayer to
Her Lord and Her God*

God, Jesus My Brother,
　　Here I sit after a night of darkness, but a sense of knowing I would go through what I needed to go through unharmed. I felt your strength guarding the door of my mind, but feelings left unguarded. I felt alone, knowing I am never alone because of Your presence but alone in this marriage. He works, makes decisions, makes money and keeps us financially stable through the work established for him, by him, but I want something more: a relationship!! This relationship is lacking, or should I say, it is with me. I can only deal with my relationship to my True Self before our marital relationship comes into play.

　　I must know what I must be to the Me, the soul as ME. This I, My God, your God Jesus and this being called Me, feels, records feelings, and this soul wants to experience the feelings that come our way to becoming Son of God. I must not only feel, but I must understand why I feel the thought and emotion that gives me the feelings. I cannot bury emotions. My soul is the essence behind my eyes, ears, touch, taste, smell, since it cannot see, so therefore needs to understand these emotions. This child inside who is blind and in darkness wants recognition. It cries, "Hey, what about 'me' in here," if not given attention. The child of my emotions must be comforted, acknowledged. It will often cry when asked to remain silent. If a child of "self condemnation" it cries out, "No more giving, tending to others, until you look at Me." I can't give it, this child, second place. Where do I fit in?

If I take the I of my being (I AM) and absorb my holiness, my rightful place here on earth, I will stop hurting, shouting, crying, and gladly emerge into the light for healing. Wholeness then is born, and I put on a new garment of clothes, and a new child is born. I cry now for what Jesus, and He responds with: "What happened with the excitement of being a traveler?" Is it guilt? The tenderness I am seeking is Me, the God within. I am God's child.

Take your cross and walk. No more are you alone.

About Ann Coon

Ann's humble view of life came out of a path of humble beginnings and a life of humbling events. She was born in the coal mining region of N.E. Pennsylvania to parents of Lithuanian descent. Her father worked the coal mines for 49 years while her mother lived and worked in the mind of what the world calls "paranoid schizophrenia."

Ann's nursing career launched her into a path of giving, loving and serving. In marriage she was given more of those gifts to love and serve. A lifetime of compassion and forgiveness and a view that love is the way to transform the world into a kinder and more gentle world so the children of the new generations can witness more peace, more love, and more compassion.

Chris and Debbie, Ann's children, have acknowledged a mother's love and she attributes that love from a loving Father God, loving Mother. Ann wishes to share a view from a child of love.

> "I'm just now beginning to understand the miracle of what you did for Debbie and me. Thank you! To be a mother, keep a house together, be a wife, hold down a career and have something left over for yourself to keep your sanity... to do all that and do them well speaks volumes to who and what you are."... **Chris**.

Ann would like to recognize the spouses of Christopher Coon and Deborah Maloy: Daina and Walter Kevin. Her five grandchildren: Zach, Jack, Josh, Elyia and Caden, are indeed members of the new generation and she gives thanks.

Ann as a child

Ann's five grandchildren (2004)

Ann's Children

Christopher and Deborah (1973)

Inspiring Thoughts

Learn to Trust Thyself Lover
*God shares his heart with us. I learn to trust
my heart to Him.*

*Keep your heart open, for it is in the open heart
that peace comes.
Hold no injustice, see that justice is served by doing good.*

*Allow the Spirit of Love to tenderize your heart.
Serving others is good.
Serve others the way you wish to be served.*

*Keep your heart alive with joy and happiness.
Knowing this the heart is well supplied.*

*Be of kind heart for that is the heart that will
attract kind heart.*

*Give God's justice where there is none;
by giving God's justice you receive God's justice.*

*Be the master of your own mind.
Your thoughts will obey you and bring you just reward.*

A Spiritual Code of Ethics

There is a child in each of us. It depends on us to determine the nature of that child; good nature or otherwise.

Be not troublesome. Do not look for trouble "out there." Seeking trouble "out there" will only find trouble within.

Do not insist on "your way," do not insist on "being right." If you are right you neighbor is seen as wrong.

Take not the truth of others as your own. You are entitled to your own truth.